MUMMY SECRETS

Bizarre Science

UNCOVERED

Ron Knapp

Enslow Publishers, Inc.
40 Industrial Road
Box 398
Berkeley Heights, NJ 07922
USA

http://www.enslow.com

Original edition published as *Mummies* in 1996.

Library of Congress Cataloging-in-Publication Data

Knapp, Ron.
  Mummy secrets uncovered / Ron Knapp.
     p. cm. — (Bizarre science)
  Includes bibliographical references and index.
  Summary: "Examines mummies, including how a mummy is formed, a history
of mummies, and examples of mummies that have been dug up around
the world, such as King Tut, Tollund Man, and the Ice Maiden"—Provided by publisher.
  ISBN 978-0-7660-3670-3
  1. Mummies—Juvenile literature. 2. Embalming—Juvenile literature. I. Title.
  GN293.K65 2011
  393'.3—dc22
                        2010000976

Paperback ISBN 978-1-59845-222-8

Printed in the United States of America

092010 Lake Book Manufacturing, Inc., Melrose Park, IL

10 9 8 7 6 5 4 3 2 1

To Our Readers: We have done our best to make sure all Internet addresses in this book were
active and appropriate when we went to press. However, the author and the publisher have no control
over and assume no liability for the material available on those Internet sites or on other Web sites they
may link to. Any comments or suggestions can be sent by e-mail to comments@enslow.com or to the
address on the back cover.

♻ Enslow Publishers, Inc., is committed to printing our books on recycled paper. The paper in every
book contains 10% to 30% post-consumer waste (PCW). The cover board on the outside of each book
contains 100% PCW. Our goal is to do our part to help young people and the environment too!

Illustration Credits: Associated Press, pp. 9, 22, 24, 35; Brian Brake / Photo Researchers, Inc., pp. 15,
16; Carlos Muñoz-Tagüe / Photo Researchers, Inc., p. 33; David Nunuk / Photo Researchers, Inc., p. 12;
dpa / Landov, p. 4; © Images & Stories / Alamy, p. 44; John G. Ross / Photo Researchers, Inc., p. 20;
© Marty Portier, p. 30; © Niels Bach, p. 37; © North Wind Picture Archives / Alamy, p. 27; RIA Novosti
/ Photo Researchers, Inc., p. 43; RIA Novosti / Science Photo Library / Photo Researchers, Inc., p. 39;
© Robert Harding Picture Library Ltd / Alamy, p. 19; Shutterstock.com, pp. 1 (background), 29, 40;
© The South Tyrol Museum of Archaeology, pp. 7, 11; Tom McHugh / Photo Researchers, Inc., p. 1
(foreground).

Cover Illustration: Tom McHugh / Photo Researchers, Inc. (Egyptian mummy, foreground);
Shutterstock.com (Egyptian pyramid artwork, background).

CONTENTS

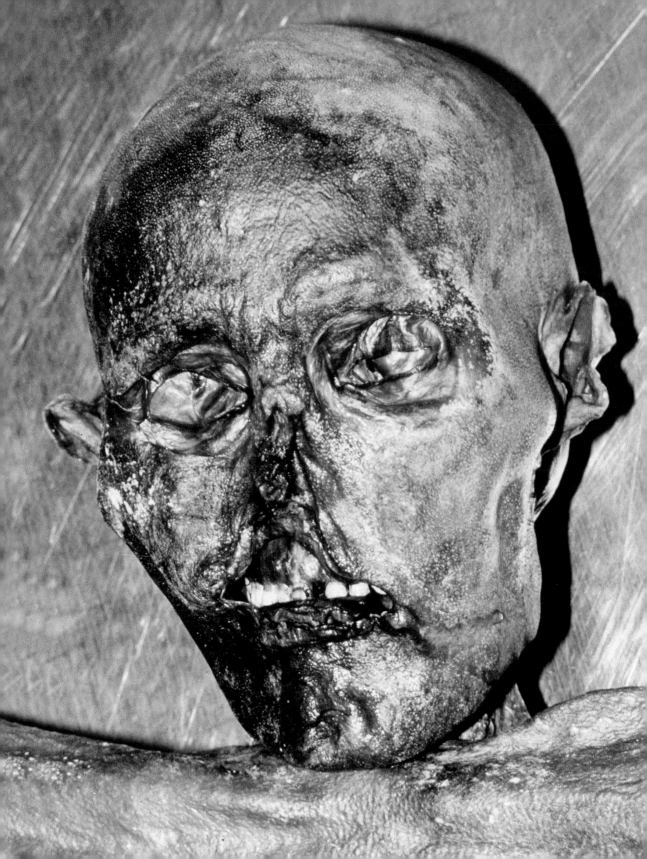

The Iceman

It was late spring. A man was moving quickly through a forest in the valleys that run north into the mountains now known as the Italian Alps. The trees in the valley had begun to sprout yellow flowers. But as the man ascended the mountains, the weather got much colder. The blooming spring trees, called hop hornbeams, disappeared.

Occasionally, the man stopped to check a wound on his hand. It was an old wound, but still caused him pain. He also listened for anyone who might be chasing him.

The hunter had been in the mountains before, and he knew how to dress. He was wearing three layers of clothes and his coat was made of deerskin. A fur hat was strapped under his chin. His leggings were made of animal skin. The grass stuffed inside his sturdy shoes with bearskin soles helped keep his feet warm.

The mummy known as the Iceman.

He had come prepared with equipment for his journey: a flint-tipped dagger, a fire-starting kit, and a birch-bark container holding embers wrapped in maple leaves. However, some of his weapons were not finished. His arrowheads were half-done and his longbow had not been strung.

As he climbed higher and higher, the wind became fierce and the pine trees provided little shelter. He reached a mountain pass at about 6,500 feet (2,000 meters) above the valley. The man stopped in a rocky hollow. Perhaps he stopped in the trench to shield himself from the wind. Maybe he was very tired from his journey. Whatever the reason, the man would remain in that trench for the next five thousand years!

Although it is unknown exactly what happened next to the man—today known as the Iceman—scientists now know he was murdered by a single stone arrow that struck his left shoulder. Minutes after the arrow hit him, the Iceman was dead.

What allows scientists to study the Iceman today? After the Iceman was murdered, the brutally cold weather in the Alps quickly covered him in snow and ice. The frigid environment kept him stuck exactly where he was, preserved under a glacier just a few feet above him.[1] Nature had created a frozen mummy!

The Iceman Is Found

The Iceman might have remained frozen forever, but in March 1991 there was a violent storm over the Sahara Desert. Dust blew north from Africa to Europe. Some of it settled on his mountain.

The dark dust absorbed much more heat from the sun than the white snow ever had. Soon the top layers of ice were melting. Finally, for the first time in fifty centuries, the sun was shining again on the Iceman.

He was found on September 19, 1991, by a pair of German mountain climbers. At first, they thought they were looking at the head and shoulders of a doll sticking out of the ice. But when they got closer, they could see that the Iceman was human. In fact, his frozen eyeballs were staring back at them.

Mountain climbers first discovered the Iceman in 1991. This is the site in the Italian Alps where the mummy was found.

At first, nobody was concerned about the body found in the ice. It wasn't unusual for skiers and climbers to get lost in the Alps. Frozen bodies were often found whenever the weather warmed and a few inches of the snow melted. The Iceman didn't appear to be anything special. He was dressed in a deerskin coat and had a fur cap over his head. On his belt was a pouch that looked a lot like a modern fanny pack.

Soon after the discovery, several hikers climbed up the mountain to have a look at the Iceman. They chopped at the ice with ski poles and axes in an attempt to free the body. While they worked, they broke the frame of his backpack and snapped his bow. Some of them ripped off pieces of his coat for souvenirs. An impatient policeman brought up a jackhammer to finish the job. It blasted away a chunk of the Iceman's hip. It took four days to get him out of the ice. During that time, the exposed parts of his body thawed out each day in the warm sun, then froze again at night.

Scientists Go to Work

Rainer Henn, a forensic expert, was probably the first to suspect that the Iceman was not just another frozen skier. "When I saw this knife," he said, "I had the idea that this man was very old." The knife had a wooden handle and a blade made out of a piece of flint more than an inch long. Flint was the rock used by many ancient peoples for arrowheads. "From that moment I ordered all the people to be most careful while getting the body out of the ice."[2] Once the body was free, it was packed in a bag

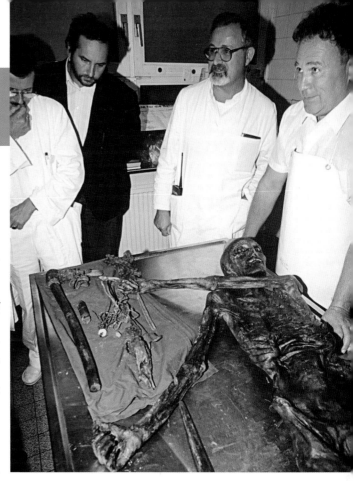

and flown to a nearby Austrian village. There, the left arm was broken when it was stuffed into a coffin for a car ride to Innsbruck. For thousands of years, the Iceman's body had been undamaged, but in four days, the rescuers had almost wrecked it.

Konrad Spindler, an archaeologist in Innsbruck, was shocked when he saw the Iceman. "I needed only one second," he said, "to see that the body was four thousand years old."[3] It was the ax that caught his attention. The four-inch blade appeared to be bronze. Leather thongs soaked in tree sap held it to the handle. Spindler knew bronze tools were used around 2000 B.C.

When the ax was examined more closely, the blade was found to be made of copper. Hot, melted liquid had been poured into a mold, then cooled and hammered into shape. Prehistoric men in Europe had used copper long before they had used bronze. The experts finally decided that the Iceman had lived around 3000 B.C. His was the oldest preserved body ever found.

Why Was the Iceman Murdered?

Evidence that the Iceman had been murdered was first discovered by Paul Gostner in June 2001. He planned to use a portable X-ray machine to examine the Iceman's broken ribs. But he discovered something that previous scientists had missed: a stone arrowhead lodged beneath the Iceman's left shoulder blade.

In 2005, a group of scientists, including Gostner, took a closer look at the body under a new CT scanning machine. The amazing results showed that the sharp piece of stone had made a half-inch gash in a major artery. This caused serious blood loss, ultimately causing his death.

Another new finding in 2007 indicated that the Iceman also suffered from head trauma, meaning he received a blow to the head. It is unclear which happened first, but the arrow wound alone would have killed him quickly.[4]

But who killed him? This will likely never be known. However, because of the copper-bladed ax the Iceman carried with him, it is believed he was an important person in his village. Also, he wore a striped goatskin shirt that researchers believe was worn by the upper classes.

One theory suggests members of a rival tribe killed him. The wound found on his hand suggests he had been in an earlier fight. The initial attack had failed, so the tribe sent men after him to finish the job. Some scientists believe that the attacker tried to cover his tracks by pulling out the arrow shaft. The attacker did not take any of the Iceman's fine possessions, because he surely

would have been identified as the killer if he were carrying them.

New theories are sure to come about. Scientists will continue to examine the Iceman. Today, the Iceman's body rests in a refrigerated chamber in a museum of archaeology in Bolzano, Italy. As new technology is introduced, scientists are able to conduct new tests on the Iceman to learn more about his life and death. The mysteries of a man who died five thousand years ago are still being unraveled.

Bodies That Don't Decay

When people and animals die, their bodies begin to decay. Bacteria breaks down the flesh and organs. After a few months, there is nothing left but bones.

Modern people have developed methods to embalm, or preserve, bodies. Blood is removed and replaced by a fluid containing formaldehyde, a chemical that prevents decay. There is nothing new about preserving bodies; people have been doing it for thousands of years. Bodies from the past that have not decayed are called mummies.

Sometimes mummies are formed naturally. If conditions are right, hot and dry air, severe cold, or bogs can preserve bodies.

Mummies can be formed naturally, like this mummy that was found in the desert highlands of southern Peru. The extremely hot and dry conditions preserved the body for about two thousands years.

Some societies have gone to a lot of trouble to create mummies. Usually for religious reasons, they want bodies to remain intact. Modern scientists have made mummies, too, combining bones and plaster.

Mummies give us unique clues to the lives and cultures of the people who came before us. By examining their teeth, scientists can determine the texture of the food they ate. Sometimes it's possible to examine their final meal by looking into what's left of their stomachs. The condition of the skin and bones reveals whether or not the person had to do tough, physical labor.

Clothing and other artifacts found with the mummies offer information as well. A type of moss found with the Iceman that may have been used as toilet paper has convinced many experts that he had come from what is now the Italian side of the Alps. That is the only place that particular moss grows. We can discover how the ancient people hunted by examining their weapons.

From carefully prepared mummies, we learn a lot about what their societies considered important. None of them would have gone to the trouble of preserving bodies if they had not believed in an afterlife. These bodies were being prepared for a new life after death. Some of the religious beliefs we discover seem strange, even troubling, to us. What kind of a god would demand human sacrifices? How could anybody believe that statues and slaughtered animals were going to come to life to serve the mummies?

We would know more about the ancient world if the first discoverers of the mummies had been more careful. Many Egyptian

Mummies and their tombs can teach us a lot about ancient cultures. In this Egyptian mural found in the tomb of Sennedjem, the god Anubis prepares the mummy of Sennedjem. Anubis was the god of mummification and afterlife in ancient Egyptian mythology.

mummies were stomped to dust or ground up to be used as medicine, or brown pigment for painting. Robbers stole almost all of the treasures left in the tombs. Even modern discoveries are sometimes damaged before scientists arrive on the scene.

The mummies and the other evidence that is left cannot answer all our questions. We're not even sure how all of them died. The search for more evidence and more answers goes on. Archaeologists around the world continue to dig for more mummies and other clues to the past. Scientists in laboratories continue to examine the ancient bodies already found.

At the same time, thousands of people view the discoveries in museums around the world. They are fascinated by the artifacts once used by ancient peoples. The mummies are always popular exhibits. History comes alive when you look into the face of somebody who's been dead for hundreds or thousands of years.

King Tut

The little boy was only nine years old. His head was shaved except for a long, thin braid that hung down his neck. Like the other boys of Egypt, he wore jeweled earrings that dangled down to his shoulders. His eyes were outlined in dark makeup. Because today was special, he wore a linen cloth wrapped tightly around his waist. Today, little Tutankhaten would become a god.[1]

Three thousand years ago, Egypt was the most powerful civilization on the earth. For centuries, the Egyptians had built pyramids, beautiful temples, and monuments along the Nile River in the middle of the desert. The country was ruled by a series of kings called pharaohs. Tutankhaten was a member of the royal family. After several relatives had died, he was next in line to the throne.

This is the gold death mask of King Tut.

At his coronation, Tut was led by priests into a huge temple. They sprinkled water from the Nile on him. They wrapped a ceremonial snake around his body. Then they set a huge crown on his head. Because a pharaoh needed a queen, he was married to Ankhesenpaaten, a girl who was probably his niece. She was only about twelve years old.

Then the little pharaoh and his queen walked out of the temple and were presented to the people of Egypt. When Tut walked into the sun, everyone in the crowd bowed low. The Egyptians believed in dozens of gods. Now that he was pharaoh, the nine-year-old boy was a god, too.

Life was good for royal Egyptian children. The boys wrestled, went swimming, and shot arrows from bows. They rolled dice and moved playing pieces around a board game called senet. Little children played with wooden spark-makers. Since he was in the royal family, Tut had learned to read and write in the complicated picture language called hieroglyphics. He also could add, subtract, and multiply.[2]

After he became pharaoh, Tutankhaten probably had no more time for senet or for playing with other boys. His days were spent with priests and tutors. When he was still young, the country was ruled by his advisers, but even they had to bow down to the little pharaoh. As Tut got older, he was given more responsibility. Soon he would be running the country on his own. As they became teenagers, Tut and Ankhesenpaaten fell in love and had at least two children. The priests convinced the royal couple to change their names to Tutankhamun and Ankhesenamun to honor the chief Egyptian god, Amon.[3]

By the time he was nineteen, Tut should have been able to look forward to growing old with his queen and their children. He wanted to keep his nation strong and happy, but suddenly he died, and Ankhesenamun married an old priest named Ay, who became the new pharaoh. Within a few generations, the boy king was almost totally forgotten.

The Pharaoh Is Found

In 1916, a British archaeologist named Howard Carter came to Egypt looking for what was left of Tutankhamun 3,200 years after the pharaoh's death. Carter knew that the ancient Egyptians had buried their pharaohs in tombs cut out of rocky hills in the desert. They surrounded the bodies with gold and jewels. The tombs

A board game called senet found in the tomb of King Tut. He probably played this game as a young boy.

The sarcophagus of King Tut in his tomb in the Valley of the Kings.

were so filled with treasures that they were targets of thieves for thousands of years. After careful study, Carter decided that the tombs of all the pharaohs except Tutankhamun had been looted thousands of years before. He was convinced that Tut was still buried in an undiscovered tomb in the Valley of the Kings.

For six years, the archaeologist and his crew carefully shifted through two hundred thousand tons of sand and stone and came up empty-handed. Then on November 4, 1922, they found a series of steps carved into the rock. Carter's workers emptied the stairway of sand and rocks and realized they had finally found the final resting place of Tutankhamun.

The tomb wasn't just a hole for the body—it was four rooms cut into the side of the hill. The rooms were filled with golden statues, chests, and beautiful vases. There was also a chariot that the king had used and the feathers of a bird he had killed while hunting. On the sides of chests and the back of a golden throne were pictures of Tut and Ankhesenamun. There was also a little chair he had used when he was a boy, as well as a toy lighter and a game of senet.

One of the rooms was filled with a wooden box covered with gold. Inside, Carter found a stone box we call a sarcophagus. When the top was removed, he found a wooden coffin, covered with gold, in the shape of a body. Inside of it was another wooden coffin, just a little smaller, but also covered with gold. Inside that one was the third and final coffin, but it wasn't made of wood. It was built out of solid gold.

Opening the Golden Coffin

Inside the third coffin, Carter finally found what he was looking for. There was the pharaoh's body wrapped in yards and yards of linen. Over the top of it was a beautiful gold death mask decorated with hundreds of jewels. Each of his fingers was wrapped in a gold tube. Daggers, rings, bracelets, collars, and jewels were wrapped in the linen that circled his body.

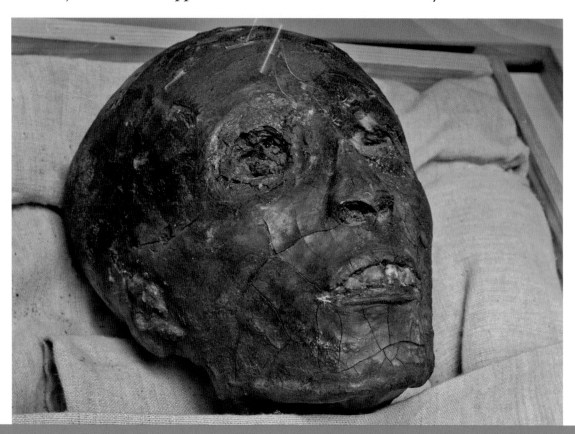

King Tut's body was a black, sticky mess after Howard Carter finished taking off the linen. The face of King Tut is seen here in a glass case in his tomb.

When Carter finished taking off all the linen, he could finally see what was left of Tutankhamun's body. The king had only been about five feet, four inches tall. His ears were pierced, and his head and chin had been carefully shaved. His liver, lungs, stomach, and intestines had been removed, dried in salts, anointed with oils, and wrapped in linen. They were found in tiny coffins in another room of the tomb. His shriveled heart was the only organ left in his body.

Tutankhamun's skin was brittle and discolored, but it was still there, and it covered his body. The Egyptians had kept the body from decomposing by storing it for two months in natron, a combination of salt and baking soda that is found naturally in Egypt. This was stuffed inside the body, too. That removed all the moisture before it was wrapped up in linen. The body would have been in much better shape if the priests had not drenched it with oils and resins that turn dark over time. Over the centuries, they had combined with the linen to make a dark, sticky mess.

The pharaoh's body was preserved because his people believed he was setting off on a long journey. He would be reborn in the land of the dead. His tomb was filled with his possessions. The rooms were stuffed full of furniture, toys, weapons, and clothes. There was even a box of loincloths. So he wouldn't be hungry, many baskets of food lined the wall. Because he would need servants in his new life, hundreds of tiny statues called ushabtis were scattered throughout the tomb. In the land of the dead, they would come to life and go to work for him.

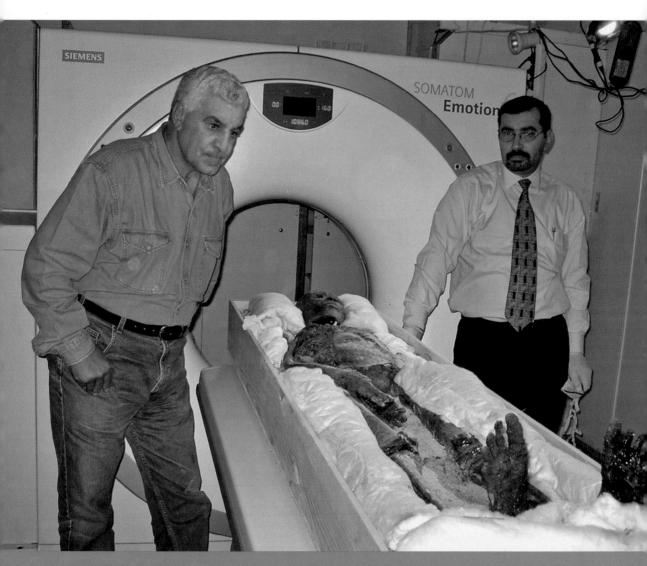

King Tut is about to be X-rayed by a CT scanning machine in this photograph taken on January 5, 2005. The CT scans proved that he had not died from a blow to the head.

The Death of a God

Tut was well prepared for the land of the dead, but how exactly did he die? In the thousands of hieroglyphics found written and carved in the tomb, there is no mention of what happened to him. Carter found a small scar on the pharaoh's cheek. Maybe he had been wounded in battle or hurt in an accident.

In 1968, further testing and modern X rays revealed something else. Tut's skull appeared to be damaged, possibly caused by something that had banged into his head. Could he have been murdered? Actually, no—CT scans taken of him in 2005 disproved this theory.

In February 2010, after two years of DNA testing and CT scans, the true reason for King Tut's death was uncovered. He died of complications from a broken leg, which was made worse by malaria. Scientists found DNA of the malaria parasite in King Tut's bones.[4] These new tests also showed that King Tut had been a frail young man, who often walked with a cane.

These new discoveries have given us a better understanding of how King Tut lived and died. New information is sure to come in the future. Meanwhile, his treasures have appeared in museums all over the world. The boy king has become the most famous ancient Egyptian of them all.

4

Victims of Vesuvius

More than nineteen hundred years ago, Pompeii was a small Roman city on the Mediterranean Sea. It was a beautiful place to live for its twenty thousand people. The weather was almost always warm and sunny. Cool breezes from the Mediterranean kept it from getting too hot. A tall mountain called Vesuvius stood about a mile away.

Perfumes, cloth, and fish sauce were made there. Farmers brought their produce to markets in the city. Ships from all over the Mediterranean landed goods at its docks. Most of the homes had two stories. Almost all of them were built around open court-yards. There was an amphitheater, temples, and gymnasiums. Many shops lined the busy stone streets.

The people of Pompeii had a good life, and they expected it to continue. Nobody suspected that they were in danger from the pretty green mountain that overlooked their city. Nobody realized that Vesuvius was actually an active volcano. It had never erupted since the town had been built.

The End of Pompeii

Then, on a summer morning in A.D. 79, the earth shook and there was a horrible noise as the top blew off Vesuvius. Smoke and ash

In this illustration, people in Pompeii run for cover from the falling rock and hot ash spitting out of Mount Vesuvius.

poured out of the broken mountain, darkening the sky. Fire was also exploding out of the giant hole. Stones so hot that they were on fire shot into the air.

Terrified people tried to save themselves. One family hid in their cellar. There, they were safe from the ash and falling rocks. But poisonous gases had begun to leak out of Vesuvius and the cracks in the ground. The people in the cellar started to faint. One of them finally realized they needed fresh air. He grabbed his key and headed for the door, but he had moved too late. He collapsed before he could open it. All eighteen people in the cellar died.

The eruption interrupted a group of priests eating a breakfast of eggs and fish. As they ran out of town, many of them were crushed by falling columns. The rest ran into a home. All but one were soon smothered by ash. As the sizzling ash seeped through one wall, the sole survivor grabbed a hatchet and cracked open the opposite wall. The ash followed, and he had to smash through another wall. He managed to stay ahead of the ash until he finally ran into a wall he couldn't break. Then he died, too.

A guard dog yanked at his chain, but he could not pull free. The poor animal choked to death as he was buried in ash.

A young girl thought the ash shower would soon end. If she could just keep it out of her nose and mouth for a few minutes, it would stop, and she would be safe. So she fell to the ground and pulled her dress up over her head, but the ash kept falling, and she was smothered.

For two days the ground shook, and Vesuvius rained death. "At last the darkness thinned. . . ." wrote a survivor. "We were terrified to see everything changed, buried deep in ashes like snowdrifts."[1] In places, the ash was thirty feet deep. Pompeii was gone.

Victims Are Forgotten

After a few years, grass and trees began growing over the city. People forgot it had ever even existed. Then, almost seventeen centuries later, in 1748, a farmer digging in a vineyard found a

Ruins of the ancient city of Pompeii with Mount Vesuvius in the background. The eruption of Vesuvius completely buried Pompeii for hundreds of years.

buried wall. Soon workers began uncovering the ancient doomed city. The work has continued now for more than two hundred fifty years. Today, the ashes have been cleared away. Visitors can walk the ancient streets and look at the many walls and columns that weren't wrecked by the eruption.

An Italian archaeologist, Giuseppe Fiorelli, was the man who made it possible for us to feel the agony of Vesuvius's victims. In 1864, he discovered that the ash had hardened around their bodies. When the bodies decayed, they had left perfect molds

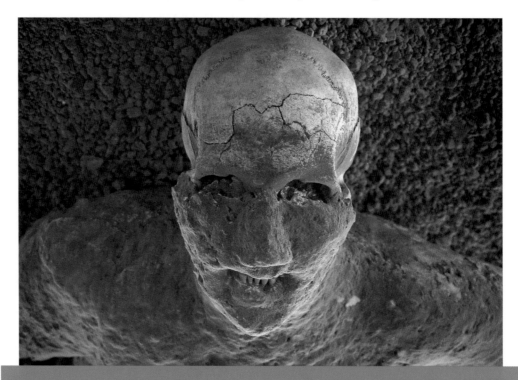

Archaeologists have made hundreds of mummies in Pompeii. Although the plaster mummies only contain bones, the expressions on their faces are very real and some still have their teeth.

surrounding their bones. Fiorelli poured plaster into the molds. When it hardened, he chipped away the ash. That left a white plaster mummy filled with bones, showing exactly how the victims had appeared when they died.

Hundreds of the mummies have been prepared by Fiorelli and more recent archaeologists. These plaster mummies aren't of as much interest to scientists as the Iceman or King Tut. The skin and organs have totally decomposed, and the bones are stuck inside the plaster. The teeth are visible on those who died gasping or screaming for breath, but no other body parts can be inspected.

What we are left with is a horrifying moment frozen forever by ash and then plaster. Although the ash destroyed a lot of information on the bodies, archaeologists are still learning about how the people lived, what they ate, and even what their gardens looked like. And we have a very accurate picture of how these unfortunate people died.

Even though they are made of plaster, the mummies of Pompeii seem more real to most of us because they look like real people. The terrified, twisted dog still seems to be struggling for his life nearly two thousand years after he died. We wish that the ash had not been as thick so that the little girl with the dress pulled over her head could have run to safety. Their mummies, and those of the people who died with them, help us to understand what it must have been like to have been in Pompeii that terrible day.

Tollund Man

It was early spring and the weather was still cool, but the man wore only a cap, a belt, and a rope around his neck. He tried not to react when the ends of the rope were twisted. He knew what was coming. The noose got tighter and tighter, and soon he was dead. Finally, the rope was loosened, and his limp body was lowered into a soggy black bog.

On May 8, 1950, two brothers, Emil and Viggo Hojgaard, were near the same spot in Tollund Fen, Denmark, digging up peat, a dark soil formed by layers of dead plants packed down in soggy ground. The brothers cut the peat into chunks so that it could be dried and then burned as fuel.

Everything was fine until they got down about seven feet. Then their spades struck something hard. Looking down, they saw the head of a dead man, wearing a cap. When police arrived at the bog, they noticed that the man's face seemed to be an unnatural reddish-brown. Tollund Man, as he would soon be known, appeared to be sleeping. The police suspected that he had recently fallen or been shoved into the bog.

A Murder Long Ago

Professor Peter Glob arrived and quickly discovered the rope wrapped around Tollund Man's neck. The ends hung down his back. It was obvious he had been killed. But who had done it? And who exactly was Tollund Man? Nobody around Tollund Fen recognized his face.

Glob took the body and the peat that surrounded it to Copenhagen's National Museum. The first thing he noticed was the man was only wearing a belt, a cap, and the rope. Not all of

Emil and Viggo Hojgaard discovered Tollund Man in a bog in Tollund Fen, Denmark. This is how Tollund Man looked when they found him.

his body was as well preserved as the head, and some of his bones were showing, but his internal organs were in great shape.

Over the next several weeks, Glob began to unravel the mystery of Tollund Man. It was obvious he wasn't accustomed to tough physical work, because his hands and feet were soft, and his fingernails weren't broken. By examining the stomach and intestines, Glob determined that Tollund Man's last meal had been a porridge made out of grains and seeds.

The condition of the teeth led the professor to believe that he was at least twenty years old. There was stubble on his chin. His hair was short—about two inches long. And it was red—just like his skin.

Glob was able to report conclusively that a murder had been committed, but he told the police not to bother looking for the murderers. The "crime" had taken place almost two thousand years before. The victim himself had probably wanted to die.[1]

The Goddess Demands a Sacrifice

Scientists initially believed Tollund Man had been placed in the bog about two thousand years ago. However, a more recent radiocarbon dating test using a small amount of his hair dates Tollund Man to around 400 B.C.[2]

At that time, the people around the Tollund bog worshiped many gods and goddesses. One of the most powerful was Nerthus, the goddess of fertility, whose symbol was a twisted rope. If she was happy, the people would have a successful harvest. But if

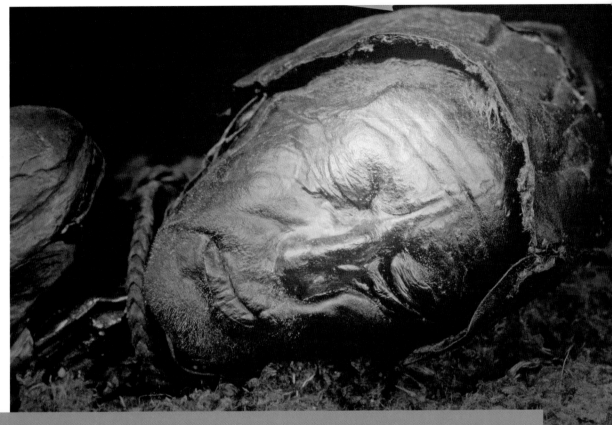

A photo of Tollund Man's body was displayed at the Mysterious Bog People exhibit at the Natural History Museum of Los Angeles County in California on March 23, 2006. The head of Tollund Man had been very well preserved in the bog.

she was angry, the crops wouldn't grow and the people might starve. Their religious customs had been described by the Roman historian Tacitus two thousand years ago.

The ancient farmers around Tollund figured they knew how to keep Nerthus happy. One of the men was picked each year to be her husband. That was why his hands were soft. He had been worshiped as a god, and he did not have to work. But at the end of a religious festival, his time was up. He was sacrificed to his "wife," Nerthus, strangled by the twisted rope that was her symbol.[3] Glob knew that bodies of other sacrificial victims had been found in Denmark and other Scandinavian countries. Many of them had also been strangled.

There were no scratches or other evidence of a struggle on Tollund Man's body. He had wanted to die. It was his duty. Besides, his was a good bargain. After being strangled, he believed that he would be with the goddess forever, and his death would guarantee a fine harvest for his people. His sacrifice would help keep them alive another year.[4]

The Bog Preserves the Body

After his death, Tollund Man's body was lowered into the sacred bog. His people had no way of knowing that burying him there would preserve his body for thousands of years. A bog is a soggy low area from which water cannot drain. Layers and layers of dead plants build up on the bottom under the water. Over the years, the plants are packed down and decay. They turn into peat, which looks like black dirt.

Moss grows over the soggy bog, trapping the water under the surface. That causes the water to lose its oxygen. The moss gives off acid that kills bacteria. Without oxygen and bacteria in the water, nothing in the bog can decay. It just turns red. The bog becomes a mummy-maker, and bodies in it can last forever.

Not All the Victims Wanted to Die

Many other bodies have been discovered in the bogs of Denmark and other European countries. Some of them apparently weren't as ready as Tollund Man to die. At least one struggled, and the rope around his neck wasn't enough to kill him. His throat was slit, and his skull was bashed in.

Today, the head of Tollund Man is on display in Silkeborg, Denmark. Visitors can come face to face with a man who died 2,400 years ago. They can look at his calm, peaceful expression and wonder if they would have had the courage to face death as he did.

This drawing shows Tollund Man eating his last meal before he was sacrificed. Scientists, by examining Tollund Man's stomach and intestines, determined that he ate porridge made from grains and seeds for his last meal.

The Ice Maiden

It was spring, time for the Pazyryks to leave the Pastures of Heaven. But first, the burial had to be completed. The ground had thawed so they could dig the pit and line it with logs. Chunks of mutton and horsemeat were left to provide nourishment on the way to the new life. The mummy itself was laid on its side in a coffin made from a hollowed log.

The body had been prepared for its journey. The skull had been opened and the brain removed. All the internal organs and muscles had been scraped away. The Pazyryks then stuffed the body with herbs, grasses, and wool, and sewed it back together.

At the edge of the pit stood six horses dressed in beautiful harnesses. The sheep, the rest of the horses, and the Pazyryks would soon be leaving for the summer pastures, but the decorated horses would not. As they waited, a strong man picked up a heavy pointed ax and walked toward them. Suddenly, he smashed it into the skull of one of the horses. One at a time, the others were killed

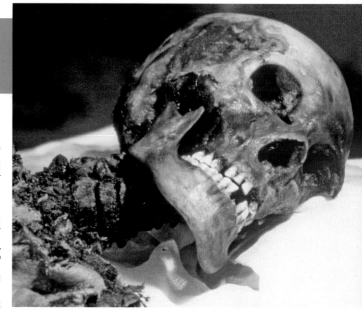

and lowered into the pit. They, too, would be needed on the way to the new life.

A wooden lid was placed over the log walls, forming a small room around the coffin. Then the pit was refilled with dirt. On top was a kurgan—a mound of rocks. The Pazyryks then left the Pastures of Heaven.

"The End of Everything"

In the summer of 1993, 2,500 years later, Natalia Polosmak, a Russian archaeologist, brought her students to the steppes of Siberia. This is an area of cold, treeless plains surrounded on three sides by China, Mongolia, and Kazakhstan. The Siberians call it Ukok, "the end of everything."[1] No roads lead to the steppes, and there are no nearby towns. The only way to get to Ukok is a five-hour helicopter ride.

Polosmak knew Ukok had once been used as winter pastures by the Pazyryks, an ancient nomadic tribe. The winter winds were so strong that they blew away all the snow, leaving bare frozen grass for their sheep to graze. The Pazyryks thought of Ukok as

A view of the Siberian steppes with mountains in the background. The Siberians call this region Ukok, "the end of everything."

the closest spot on the world to heaven. They called the area "the Pastures of Heaven."

Polosmak led her crew to a kurgan. Under the mound of rocks, she expected to find at least traces of a Pazyryk burial chamber. Since the kurgans were so visible, she knew that many of them had been looted by tribes that came later. This time she was lucky. When the rocks and dirt were cleared away, there was the unbroken lid of a chamber. No one had been inside for twenty-five centuries!

The archaeologist knew the most she could expect to find was a skeleton and a few artifacts. When the lid was removed, all she could see was ice. Sometime after the burial, the entire chamber had filled with water that was still frozen. If the chamber had been soaked in water for any length of time, almost everything inside would probably be ruined.

Polosmak wondered when the water had entered the chamber. If it had leaked in soon after the burial and frozen quickly, everything inside would be very well preserved. She realized there wasn't much chance of the crew being that lucky.

The Ice Melts

With the lid off, the sun warmed the chamber for the first time in centuries. Soon, the ice began turning into mush. To speed the melting, Polosmak poured hot water onto the ice. Soon she could see a long wooden coffin, then two small tables holding mutton and horsemeat. Since the food hadn't completely rotted away, Polosmak knew it must have frozen very quickly after the burial. As the hot water hit the meat, it formed a kind of hot soup. Polosmak could smell the 2,500-year-old meal.

As the deeper ice turned to mush, she could see the rotting bodies of the six horses. Pieces of their brown coats still hung to their bones. Each of them had a hole in its skull made by the blow of the ax. Soon their thawed bodies began to stink in the sun.

Polosmak turned her attention to the coffin. When long bronze nails were pulled out, the lid could be removed. Inside was a solid block of dark ice. She wondered what would be left of the dead Pazyryk. She knew the body would have been damaged when the skull was split and the organs removed, but she hoped that what was left hadn't had a chance to decompose before freezing.

As she poured hot water from a cup onto the ice inside the coffin, the archaeologist began to see shapes emerge. The first thing she recognized was a jawbone. Then, as more of the ice melted, a chunk of flesh on a cheek was revealed.

Soon, the whole mummy was free of ice, and Polosmak could see it was covered by a fur blanket. When she pulled back the blanket she could see the body wore a flowing woolen skirt and a silk tunic. It also had a long wooden headdress decorated by eight carved cats covered with gold. The mummy had been a noble woman. She has since been named the Ice Maiden.[2]

Much of the body was still covered by soft skin. Her long fingers looked like they belonged on the body of a strong young woman, not on someone who had been dead for 2,500 years. When Polosmak pulled the blanket back from one of the hands, she found a dark blue tattoo of a deer on the Ice Maiden's wrist. Under the tunic was another tattoo on her shoulder. It was a strange design of a mythical creature with long, swirling horns.

Polosmak knew she had been very lucky. The Ice Maiden's burial chamber had obviously been flooded by rain or melting snow soon after it had been sealed. Almost immediately, the water had frozen, preserving what was left of the horses, the meal, and the Ice Maiden.

Who Was She?

The archaeologist decided she must have been very important to her people. Why else would she have been given such a special burial? The Pazyryks could not have left six horses in the tombs of every dead member of the tribe. The Ice Maiden must have done something very special to deserve such treatment.

There are still questions about the tomb in the Pastures of Heaven. What was the meaning of the tattoos? Was the headdress

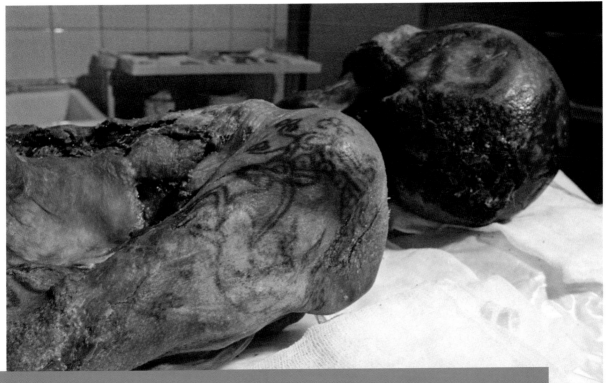

The Ice Maiden's tattoo of the mythical creature on her shoulder is shown in this photo. Despite 2,500 years underground, the Ice Maiden's skin had been so well preserved that the tattoos are still clearly visible.

These two women are dressed in the ancient Pazyryk manner. The original clothes were found in the kurgans of the Ukok Plateau in the Siberian steppes. It is possible that the Ice Maiden wore this type of clothing.

some kind of crown? How had the Ice Maiden died? Polosmak admitted, "What we know is not everything."[3]

A helicopter carried the Ice Maiden from Ukok to Moscow, Russia, where scientists investigated the mummy. Natalia Polosmak's discovery pieced together more information about the history of the Pazyryks. She and other Russian scientists wished to do further digging in Ukok. But Russian archaeologists are no longer allowed to dig on the high plateau of the Ice Maiden's final resting place. Some did not want the sacred burial ground disturbed. The battle over this continues as the Altai people, descendants of the Pazyryks, wish to have the Ice Maiden's body reburied.[4]

The discovery of the Ice Maiden, like many other mummies uncovered around the world, gives us a glimpse into cultures of the past, unlocking secrets buried thousands of years ago.

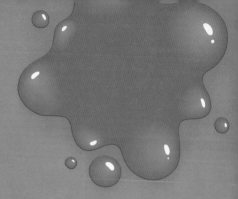

CHAPTER NOTES

Chapter 1. The Iceman

1. Stephen S. Hall, "Iceman Mystery," *National Geographic*, September 2007, <http://ngm.nationalgeographic.com/2007/07/iceman/hall-text/1> (January 7, 2010).
2. Sandy Fritz, "Who Was the Iceman?" *Popular Science*, vol. 242, no. 2 (February 1993), p. 46.
3. David Roberts, "The Ice Man: Lone Visitor From the Copper Age," *National Geographic*, vol. 184, no. 6 (June 1993), p. 47.
4. John Roach, "Head Trauma Contributed to Iceman's Demise," *National Geographic News*, August 31, 2007, <http://news.nationalgeographic.com/news/2007/08/070831-iceman-death.html> (January 7, 2010).

Chapter 3. King Tut

1. Christiane Desroches-Noblecourt, *Tutankamen* (Boston: New York Graphic Society, 1976), p. 170.
2. Cyril Aldred, *Tutankhamen's Egypt* (New York: Charles Scribners' Sons, 1972), p. 46.
3. I. E. S. Edwards, *The Treasures of Tutankhamun* (Middlesex, U.K.: Penguin Books, Ltd., 1972), p. 18.
4. Paul Schemm, "A frail King Tut died from malaria, broken leg," *San Francisco Chronicle*, February 16, 2010, <http://www.sfgate.com/cgi-bin/article.cgi?f=/n/a/2010/02/16/international/i065807S49.DTL> (February 18, 2010).

Chapter 4. Victims of Vesuvius

1. Ron and Nancy Goor, *Pompeii: Exploring a Roman Ghost Town* (New York: Thomas Y. Crowell, 1986), p. ix.

Chapter 5. Tollund Man

1. P. V. Glob, "Lifelike Man Preserved 2,000 Years in Peat," *National Geographic*, vol. 105, no. 3 (March 1954), p. 419.
2. Susan K. Lewis, "Tollund Man," NOVA: The Perfect Corpse, *PBS.org*, January 2006, <http://www.pbs.org/wgbh/nova/bog/toll-flash.html> (January 7, 2010).
3. Maurice Shadbolt, "Who Killed the Bog Men of Denmark? And Why?" *Reader's Digest*, vol. 110, no. 662 (June 1977), p. 204.
4. Glob, p. 428.

Chapter 6. The Ice Maiden

1. Natalia Polosmak, "A Mummy Unearthed From the Pastures of Heaven," *National Geographic*, vol. 186, no. 4 (October 1994), p. 87.
2. "Ice Mummies: Siberian Ice Maiden," NOVA Transcripts, *PBS.org*, air date November 24, 1998, <http://www.pbs.org/wgbh/nova/transcripts/2517siberian.html> (January 8, 2010).
3. "Ice Tombs of Siberia," *National Geographic Explorer*, TBS, originally broadcast October 9, 1994.
4. Julius Strauss, "Ice Maiden Triggers Mother of all Disputes in Siberia," *Telegraph*, April 17, 2004, <http://www.telegraph.co.uk/news/worldnews/europe/russia/1459530/Ice-Maiden-triggers-mother-of-all-disputes-in-Siberia.html> (January 8, 2010).

GLOSSARY

archaeologist—A scientist who studies past human cultures and civilizations.

bog—Wet, spongy ground that usually forms when decaying plant growth fills in a swamp.

coronation—The official ceremony crowning a ruler.

CT scan—A series of detailed pictures of areas inside a body taken by a computer linked to an X-ray machine.

decompose—To decay.

embalm—To preserve a human body.

forensics—Investigation through medical examinations.

formaldehyde—A chemical used to preserve the bodies of the dead.

glacier—In cold climates, snowfall builds up creating a year-round mass of ice, especially on mountaintops.

hieroglyphics—A form of writing that uses pictures to symbolize words and sounds.

longbow—A large bow, often up to six feet in length.

malaria—A disease spread by mosquitoes that can cause death.

mutton—The meat of an older sheep.

Nerthus—An ancient fertility goddess of the Celtic people of Europe.

nomad—People, or animals, that regularly travel from place to place in search of food and shelter.

Pazyryks—An ancient nomadic people of Central Asia.

peat—The remains of plants that have decayed and become compacted beneath a swamp.

pharaoh—The name given to the male rulers of ancient Egypt.

sarcophagus—A large stone coffin.

senet—A game of the ancient Egyptians.

tunic—A loose-fitting slip-on garment, worn by ancient peoples, especially the Romans and Greeks.

ushabtis—Tiny statues placed in Egyptian tombs. In the afterlife, they were supposed to come to life to work for the mummy in the Land of the Dead.

FURTHER READING

Books

Deem, James M. *Bodies From the Ice: Melting Glaciers and the Recovery of the Past*. Boston: Houghton Mifflin, 2008.

Grace, N. B. *Mummies Unwrapped!: The Science of Mummy-Making*. New York: Franklin Watts, 2008.

Harrison, Paul. *Uncovering Mummies and Other Mysteries of the Ancient World*. Mankato, Minn.: Capstone Press, 2010.

Hawass, Zahi. *Tutankhamun: The Mystery of the Boy King*. Washington, D.C.: National Geographic, 2005.

Markle, Sandra. *Outside and Inside Mummies*. New York: Walker & Co., 2005.

Woog, Adam. *Mummies*. San Diego, Calif.: ReferencePoint Press, 2009.

Internet Addresses

Cyber Mummy
<http://archive.ncsa.illinois.edu/Cyberia/VideoTestbed/Projects/Mummy/mummyhome.html>

Mummy Tombs
<http://www.mummytombs.com/>

Nova Online—Ice Mummies
<http://www.pbs.org/wgbh/nova/icemummies/>

INDEX

A

Ankhesenamun
(Ankhesenpaaten),
18, 19, 21
arrowheads, 6, 8, 10
ax, 8, 9, 10, 38, 41

B

bogs, 13, 32, 34, 36
bronze tools, 9

C

Carter, Howard, 19–25
CT scans, 10, 25

D

DNA testing, 25

E

Egypt
civilization of, 17
King Tut
(Tutankhamun),
17–25
treatment of
mummies in, 14–15
embalming, 13

F

Fiorelli, Giuseppe,
30–31
flint knife, 6, 8
formaldehyde, 13

G

Glob, Peter, 33–36
Gostner, Paul, 10

H

Henn, Rainer, 8
hieroglyphics, 18, 25
Hojgaard, Emil and
Viggo, 32
human sacrifice, 14,
34–36

I

Ice Maiden, 38–44
Iceman, 5–11, 14

K

King Tut
(Tutankhamun),
17–25
kurgan, 39, 40

L

looting, 15, 21, 40

N

natron, 23
Nerthus, 34–36

P

Pastures of Heaven,
38–40, 43
Pazyryks, 38–44
pharaohs, 17–25
poisonous gases, 28
Polosmak, Natalia,
39–44
Pompeii, 26–31
preservation of bodies
bogs in, 36
Egyptian style of, 23

overview, 13–14
Pazyryks, 38–42
reasons for, 14, 23
temperature in, 6,
13, 41
volcanic ash, 28–31

R

radiocarbon dating, 34

S

sarcophagus, 21
Spindler, Konrad, 9
study of mummies,
benefits of, 14–15

T

tattoos, 42
Tollund Man, 32–37
tombs, 15, 19–21, 23,
25, 43

U

Ukok, 39–40, 44
ushabtis, 23

V

Vesuvius, 26–31
volcanic ash, 28–31